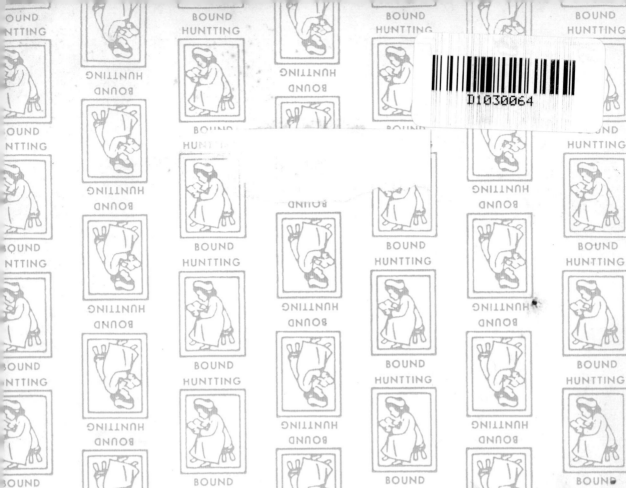

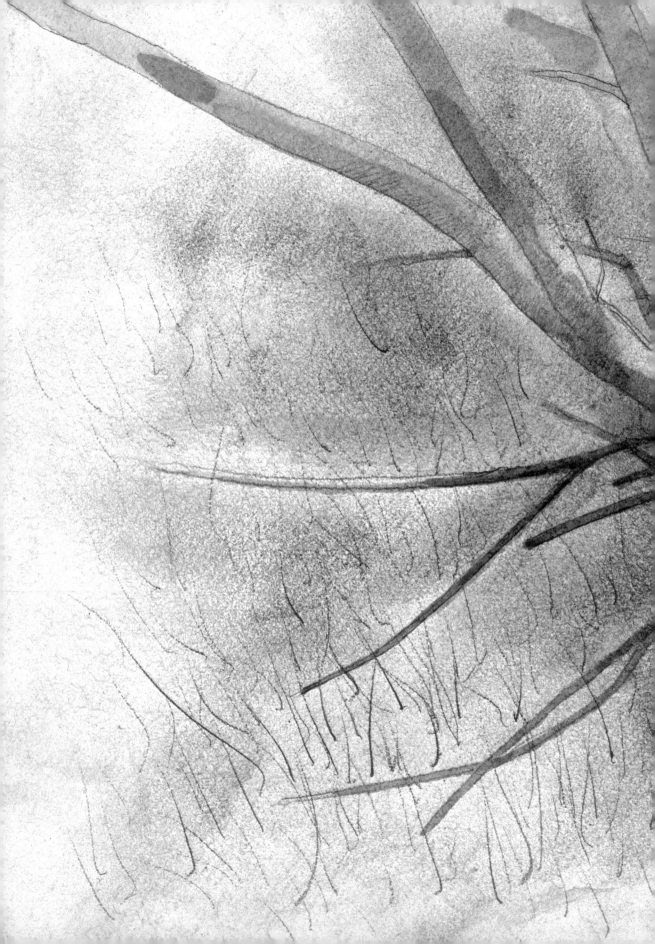

Sing,
Little Mouse

Sing,
Little Mouse

by Aileen Fisher

illustrated by Symeon Shimin

THOMAS Y. CROWELL COMPANY   NEW YORK

To Phyl and Rod
and their unexpected
visitor in fur

MANUFACTURED IN THE UNITED STATES OF AMERICA

L. C. Card 68-11061

1   2   3   4   5   6   7   8   9   10

Sing,
Little Mouse

I asked my mother,
when summer was going
and tinges and fringes
of fall were showing . . .

I asked if ever
she'd chanced to hear
a little mouse sing
in the cool of the year
in a birdlike voice
that was sweet and clear.

"A little mouse *sing!*"
She shook her head
as a leaf dropped down
that was gold and red.

"Josie," I said,
"and Jerry, too,
told me that someone
their uncle knew
had a singing mouse.
Do you think it's true?"

"A mouse that can sing
is news to me,"
she said as the west wind
shook the tree.

I asked my mother
if she could say
where a mouse
with a musical voice
might *stay*.

She said, "I hope
it will stay away."

"I wish," I sighed,
"I could hear one sing,
a gay little
gray little
velvety thing,
in summer or winter
or fall or spring.

"Does it chirp?
Does it cheep
with a bird-sounding deep?

"Does it twit?
Does it trill
in a voice that is shrill,
a velvety mouse
with a house near a hill?"

I asked my brother
who's eight years older
on a day when the sun
had a cloud on its shoulder . . .

I asked my brother . . .

And he said, "*Spring*
is the time of year
for a thing to sing.
So why not wait
till the cowslips slip
and the bluebells ring
and the catnips nip
and the dogwoods bark
in the woods and park?"

I laughed and said
I didn't see how
I could wait till spring
for a wish *right now.*

So I asked my father.
I ran to the gate
when he came home
from the office, late.

I asked my father
where I could find
the right little mouse
of a singing kind
with a twittery voice
and a musical mind.

"A mouse?" asked Father.
"That sings? Now, wait.
I'll need some time
to investigate.

"I'll need," said Father,
"a day or two
to gather some facts
and report to you.

"An astonishing thing
for a mouse to sing!"

So while I waited
I went to the store
where a sign with a puppy
hangs over the door,
and you can buy hamsters
and lovebirds and fishes
and turtles and kittens
and dog pans and dishes
and muzzles and leashes
and cockers and cages
and collars and brushes
for pets of all ages.

I said to the man:
"The particular thing
I'm eager to hear
is a little mouse sing."

The man said slowly,
"I much regret . . .
a mouse that can sing
I've never heard yet,

"But a sweet-singing bird
makes a wonderful pet,

"Or a kitten that purrs
might be better to get."

But I'd rather hear a *mouse*.

"Sing, little mouse!"
I wished twice over,
walking home
past some autumn clover.
"Sing me a mouse song
in my ear,
so I can know
if you're somewhere near."

But all I heard
was a truck appear.

Then Father came home
with a big thick book
and opened to MICE
and said, "Now, look,
with so many mice
and so many choices
we ought to find *some*
with singing voices.

"First, here's a mouse
who lives in a house.

"But your mother, I fear,
would never agree
to a House Mouse near
for us all to hear
and herself to see,
no matter how clear
its voice might be.

"Next comes a mouse
who can't be beat
when it comes to jumps.
He may jump *ten feet*.
With a long, long tail
and hind feet, too,
he jumps like a wisp
of a kangaroo.

"But cold is hard
on the little sprinter.
A Jumping Mouse sleeps
from fall through winter."

"And then does he sing,"
I asked, "in spring?"

"It seems he doesn't.
There isn't a clue . . .
except for a high-pitched
squeak or two,"
my father said
when the page was through.

"Next comes a mouse . . .
a sort of freak . . .
who wears his pockets
outside each cheek,
instead of closed in
like most of his kin.

"He lives in deserts
and hot dry plains
and stuffs his pockets
with seeds and grains."

"And makes up songs
with his Pocket-Mouse brains?"

"That's more," said Dad,
"than the book explains.

"Now here's a mouse
of another sort—
a Meadow Mouse
with a tail that's short,
and very small ears,
but no report
that it sings for practice
or sings for sport.
It seems he's not
of the singing sort.

"And here's the daintiest
mouse of all—
a white-footed Deer Mouse,
halfway small,
with a fawn-brown back,
all neatly dressed
in white silk gloves
and a white silk vest.

"With very big ears
and big black eyes,
it's a bit like a deer
in a mouse's size."

I asked my father
the same, same thing:
"Does a white-footed,
light-footed
Deer Mouse sing?"

My father read
(and he stressed each word):
"*A White-Footed Mouse
is sometimes heard
to sing a song
like a trilling bird.*"

Like a trilling bird!

"Does it say
where a mouse
like that might stay,
who would sing like a bird
on a windless day?"
I asked. "In a place
not far away?"

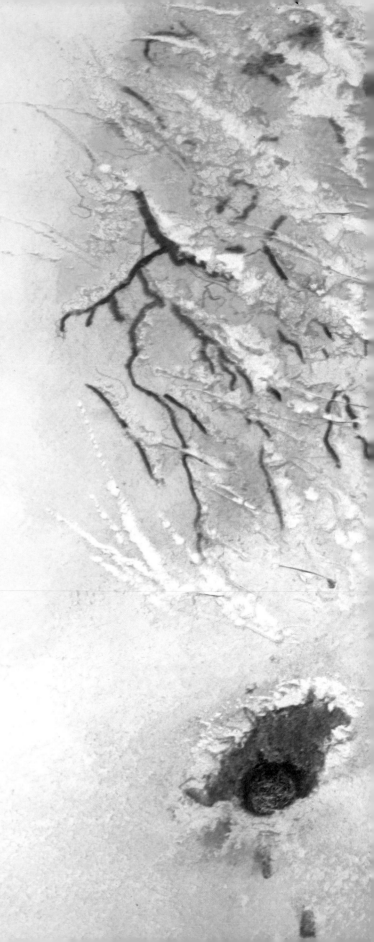

Then Father showed me
the page where one
made tracks in the snow
on a moonlight run,
with delicate footprints
small and neat
and the mark of its tail
between its feet.

And Father said, "Watch
for the tracks, and then
you'll know where to look
when it's spring again."

So after a snow,
at the end of town
where a hill went up
and a woods came down,
I found a trail
that I knew was right,
with the mark of the tail
in plainest sight.

"Mouse," I said,
"do you live in a neat
little ball of grass?
Do you hear my feet
when my snowsteps pass
on top of your street?

"Where do you go
beneath the snow?
Sing, little Deer Mouse,
so I'll know.
Sing!

"Do you sing for your supper
like little Tom Tucker?
And what do you eat
for 'white bread and butter'?
A seed that is sweet,
or a seed with a pucker?
A 'cicle of ice
for an all-day sucker?"

I stood by his hole
and listened to hear
if the song of a mouse
could find my ear,
but all I heard
(from a snow-trimmed tree)
was a black-capped bird
sing, "Chick-a-dee-dee."

A singing mouse
I never did hear
when winter was white
and cold and clear.

And then . . . one night
in the spring of the year
my brother and I
went out to listen
where starlight spattered
the pond with glisten.

The air was full
of singing and ringing,
of wonderful news
the frogs were bringing
that winter was over
and spring was springing
out of the earth
and out of the sky.

But nary a mouse song
drifted by.

My brother said
he thought he knew why.
Mice, he fancied,
might be like bats,
squeaking in high-pitched
sharps and flats
that nobody hears
with low-pitched ears.

"Though sometimes maybe
a mouse sings low,"
he said, "so we hear
how the warbles go."

I sighed, "With bullfrogs
so loud in spring
there isn't much chance
for mice that sing."

And so he promised,
"Here's what we'll do
when frogs are quiet
and peepers, too—
we'll both go back
where you saw the track
and listen and listen
the whole night through."

And that's what we did
when June grew old . . .

We took our knapsacks
with all they'd hold,
and sleeping bags
(if the night turned cold),
and off we walked
to the end of town
where a hill went up
and the woods came down.

We sat and listened.

Mosquitoes buzzed.

A half-moon glistened,
and then it fuzzed.

The grass and clover
turned damp and chilly.
But where was a mouse
whose song was trilly?

"Sing, little mouse!"
I begged inside.
"Sing, little mouse,
don't run and hide."

I crawled in my bag
for a warmer place,
with a dangle of leaves
above my face
and peanuts handy
to eat . . . in case . . .

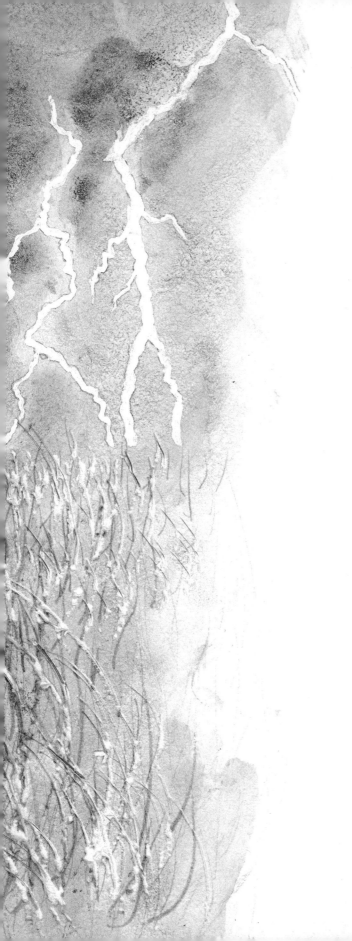

Then all of a sudden
around the sky
a thundery rumble
and roar went by,
and my brother woke up,
and so did I.

We picked up our gear,
and away we ran,
and we just reached home
when the rain began.

We dropped our things
in the downstairs hall
and tiptoed to bed
with sounds so small
you hardly could call them
sounds at all.

And then when I went
downstairs next day
to pick up my things
to put away . . .
Can you think,
can you guess
what I'm going to say?

Can you guess what I saw
in my very own house?

A White-Footed Mouse!

He must have crawled
in my bag, in under,
when clouds came up
and it looked like thunder.

And now he sat
with a nut to eat
and white silk gloves
on his hands and feet
and a white silk vest
all glossy and neat.

We made him a cage,
my brother and I.
(My mother agreed
it was safe to try.)
We put in some hay
where a mouse could hide
and a cardboard tube
he could crawl inside,
and plenty to eat,
and a wheel to ride,
and I listened,
and listened,
with both ears wide . . .

But the mouse didn't sing.

"He's probably scared,"
my father said,
"away from his nest
and his own soft bed."

"He's probably sad,"
said Mom to me,
"shut up in a cage,
no longer free."

I listened each night
for all that week.
He didn't twitter
or even *squeak*.

So I made him a promise:
"Sing for me
and I'll take you back
and I'll set you free
in your own little place
at the end of town
where the woods go up
and the hill comes down.

"Give me my wish
and sing a song
and I'll take you back
where you most belong."

And that was the night he sang!

He trilled
and twittered
as sweet and clear
as the trilliest bird
you ever did hear.

He chirred
and chittered
as soft and sweet
as the chirriest bird
you ever did meet.

I called my brother
on tiptoe feet.

I called my mother
and father to hear
the little mouse sing
in the green of the year.

And early next morning
just we two
went back to the place
that both of us knew,
and I opened the cage
and set him free.

He'd made my wishing
come true for me.

Away he ran
in his white silk vest
and his white silk gloves
to his secret nest
under the tangles
that grew nearby,
and I hoped that his ears
could hear me cry:

"Thanks, little mouse.
We won't deny
we're both of us glad
to say good-bye:

"You're free again,
and away you go . . .
and I've had my wish
so at last I know
that it's a perfectly
possible thing
for a light-footed
flight-footed
left-footed
right-footed
White-Footed Mouse
to *sing*."

ABOUT THE AUTHOR

Since the day when her first verse was printed in a local newspaper in Iron River, Michigan, Aileen Fisher has written an extraordinary number of poems, stories, and plays—mostly for children. She adheres to a stringent writing schedule, finding time as well for hiking on mountain trails and working on the 200-acre ranch she owns with a friend.

Miss Fisher lives in a cabin on the ranch in the foothills of the Rockies near Boulder, Colorado. Not only did she help to build the cabin, but she also worked on its furniture and sandstone fireplace. The cabin is lighted by kerosene, and water is pumped in by a gasoline motor.

Poetry is Miss Fisher's first love; natural history, her second. In an interview she noted that "because of the role of science in today's work . . . there is greater need than ever before to help the child understand his environment through poetry."

Miss Fisher attended the University of Chicago and later received a degree in journalism from the University of Missouri. She lived and worked in Chicago for five years before moving to the quiet beauty of Colorado.

ABOUT THE ARTIST

Symeon Shimin was born in Astrakhan, on the Caspian Sea, in Russia, and came to the United States with his family ten years later. He attended art classes at Cooper Union in the evenings, and painted for a while in the studio of George Luks. Primarily self-taught, Mr. Shimin for the most part gained his schooling in the museums and art galleries of this country and in France and Spain.

In 1938, Symeon Shimin was chosen to paint a mural in the Department of Justice Building in Washington, D.C. Recognition and many invitations to exhibit in museums followed this assignment. Mr. Shimin's paintings are in private collections, and have been shown at such museums as the Whitney Museum of Art, the Art Institute of Chicago, and the National Gallery in Washington, D.C.